If Towns Could Talk
How British Towns Grew

by Tony Fisher

Contents

What is a town?	2
Why did towns and cities begin?	4
Why have towns and cities grown?	6
Why did Melton Mowbray grow?	8
Why did Glasgow grow?	10
Why did Bradford grow?	12
Why did Canterbury grow?	14
Why did Bath grow?	16
Why did Blackpool grow?	18
Why did Blaenavon grow?	20
Why did Crewe grow?	22
Why did Cambridge grow?	24
Why did Milton Keynes grow?	26
How to be a town detective	28
Summary	30
Glossary	31
Index	32

What is a town?

Towns and cities are places where people live and work, go to school, go shopping, or go out to have fun. Millions of people in Britain live in them. All towns are different, but all towns have things in common. If towns could talk, what would they say?

All towns have:
- homes
- schools
- shops
- doctors
- roads and traffic
- jobs
- churches

Only some towns have:
- a hospital
- a local radio station
- a university
- docks
- museums
- a railway station
- a theatre
- an airport
- factories
- mosques, synagogues, temples and other different places of worship

Why did towns and cities begin?

Until about two hundred years ago most people in Britain lived in villages. There were some towns and cities as well, but they were much smaller than they are today.

But why were there towns in the first place?

Some towns began as small villages over a thousand years ago. Most of the people who lived in these villages were farmers. Some farmers grew more food than they needed. Some people did other jobs, such as make pots or cloth.

Markets began where farmers came to sell their extra food, and to buy things they needed. The potters and **weavers** bought food from the farmers and sold their pots and cloth. A town grew up around the market.

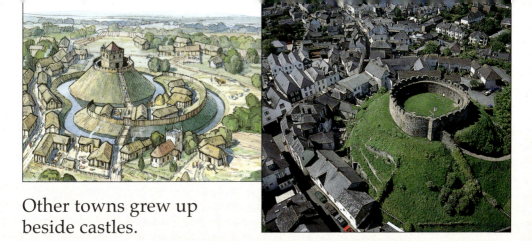

Other towns grew up beside castles.

Other towns grew up beside harbours.

All the people who lived in these towns needed the same four things:

- food
- fresh water
- building materials (wood, stone and clay)
- a supply of fuel (such as wood for heat and cooking)

These things had to be nearby, because it was difficult to transport them.

Why have towns and cities grown?

Towns in Britain have grown for many different reasons over hundreds of years. Here are some of the reasons:

- markets (see pages 8–9)
- ports (see pages 10–11)
- industry: wool (see pages 12–13)
- religion: a cathedral (see pages 14–15)
- health: spas (see pages 16–17)
- tourism: seaside (see pages 18–19)
- mining: coal (see pages 20–21)
- transport: railways (see pages 22–23)
- learning: university (see pages 24–25)
- planning: new towns (sees pages 26–27)

Some towns began growing for one reason, and then kept growing for other reasons.

If towns could talk, they would tell us interesting stories! In most towns we can find clues which help us to discover how and why they grew.

Why did Melton Mowbray grow?

Melton Mowbray

Melton Mowbray is a **market town** in Leicestershire. It is mostly surrounded by farmland.

Between 1250 and 1350 there were lots of sheep farmers living there, and lots of sheep producing lots of wool. The farmers sold the wool to wool **merchants** in the town, who then sold it to other people and became rich. Some of the wool merchants became so rich that they could afford to build big houses. Melton Mowbray became a market, not only for wool but for other goods as well.

Market

So the markets at Melton Mowbray are a clue to why the town grew. There has been a market there for over nine hundred years, and it is still a market town today. Farmers go to sell animals at the cattle market every Tuesday, and there is also a market every Saturday.

Why did Glasgow grow?

Glasgow

Glasgow is a big city in Scotland. In its early days it was a small village beside the River Clyde where people could fish for salmon. The river is a clue to why Glasgow grew.

Glasgow is on the western side of Scotland. When Britain started to import food and other **goods** like sugar, rum and tobacco from the West Indies and America, Glasgow was one of the main ports where those goods came into the country. The goods were then carried along the River Clyde and to the rest of Britain.

An aerial view of the Clyde.

When coal and **iron ore** were found nearby, iron- and steel-making began. Some of the iron was used to make great ships at shipyards along the River Clyde. As industry grew in the nineteenth century, thousands of people came to Glasgow looking for work.

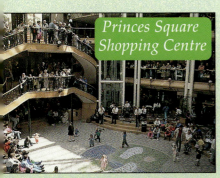

Princes Square Shopping Centre

One of the main reasons why Glasgow grew was because it was a port. Nowadays fewer **Glaswegians** earn their living by building ships, or by working at the port, but there are other industries, and other reasons why people want to live and work in Glasgow.

Glasgow Clyde Auditorium

Port

Why did Bradford grow?

Bradford is a city in Yorkshire. It started out as a Saxon village called Broadford, because it was at a **ford** where a river could be crossed.

In 1800, Bradford was a small town with a population of about sixteen thousand people. The most important local industry was wool. There were lots of **spinners** and weavers, who worked at their homes in cottages and farms. There were no factories.

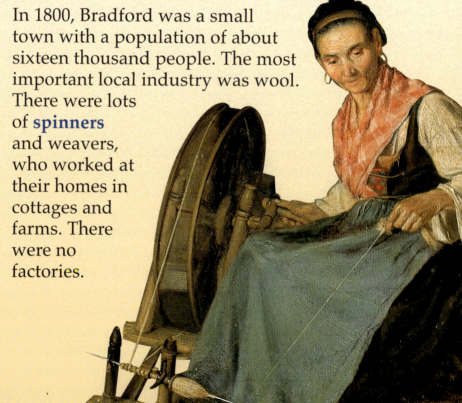

Then weaving machines were invented. Factories and mills were built, where woollen cloth was made with new machines. Many people came to Bradford to work in the woollen mills. By 1850 there were about one hundred thousand people living in Bradford. At that time Bradford was called "the wool capital of the world".

So the main reason why Bradford grew into a town was because of the growth of the woollen industry. Now the woollen industry is not as important as it once was, and the mills have closed down. But some of the old mill buildings are still there, and they give us a clue about Bradford's history.

Industry: wool

Why did Canterbury grow?

In prehistoric times people lived in villages in the area where Canterbury is today. When the Romans invaded Britain, they built a town at Canterbury. This town was later left in ruins, but a Saxon village was built in the same place.

In AD 602 a **monastery** was built at the village. The monastery became a **cathedral**, and Canterbury became the centre of the Christian religion in England. The cathedral is a big clue in the story of why Canterbury grew.

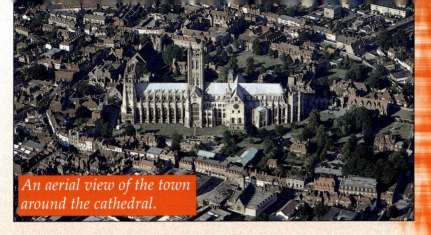
An aerial view of the town around the cathedral.

Stonemasons and other craftspeople who helped to build the cathedral lived in the growing town. In 1171 Thomas Becket, who was Archbishop of Canterbury, was murdered in the cathedral. He was made a saint, and after that, thousands of **pilgrims** came to Canterbury each year in memory of him. They needed food and places to sleep, so **inns** were built for them to stay in, and the town continued to grow.

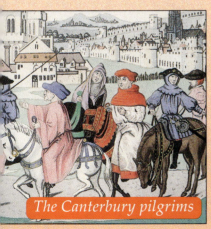
The Canterbury pilgrims

So the main reason why Canterbury grew all those years ago was because of religion. Later on, it became a **market town**. Nowadays two million tourists visit Canterbury every year and most of them visit the cathedral. These visitors need hotels, restaurants and shops. Like the pilgrims, they bring a lot of business to Canterbury.

Religion: a cathedral town

Why did Bath grow?

Bath is a city in Somerset. In the centre of the city is a building called the Pump Room. The Pump Room was built on top of the ruins of some Roman buildings, which included some public baths. The Pump Room and the Roman baths are clues to why Bath grew. The baths were built because there were hot water springs underground, and the Romans believed that the spring water made people healthy.

In 1574 Queen Elizabeth I visited Bath. After that, lots of rich people wanted to visit because of the hot springs. They needed places to stay and food to eat, so inns were built where they could stay.

A town which people visit because it is good for their health is called a **spa**. Bath became such a fashionable place that rich people wanted to live there. Many fine houses were built in Bath in the 1700s.

So one of the main reasons why Bath grew was because it was a spa. Today many tourists visit Bath to see the Roman remains and the fine houses. The town is a **World Heritage Site** because it has so many beautiful buildings.

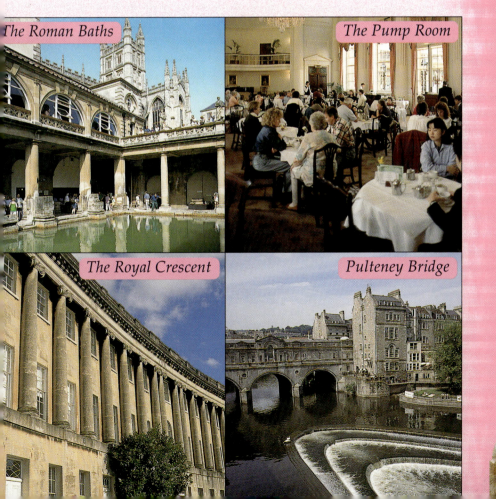

The Roman Baths

The Pump Room

The Royal Crescent

Pulteney Bridge

Health: a spa town

Why did Blackpool grow?

Blackpool

Blackpool is a town in Lancashire. If you visit Blackpool the main clue about why it grew is right in front of you. Blackpool grew because it is at the seaside!

The land around Blackpool was marshy, and the first buildings were little huts beside a stream. By 1780 some of the land had been drained, and four hotels and four **alehouses** had been built.

In 1800 only 473 people lived there, but by 1900 the population was 47,348. The main reason why Blackpool grew so quickly was because the seaside became a very popular place to go on holiday. Places were built for the visitors to stay.

Blackpool beach in 1903.

After the railways were built, the seaside attracted thousands of visitors from the **industrial towns** in Lancashire and Yorkshire. Working people came to relax and enjoy themselves beside the sea. The famous Blackpool Tower and the piers were built to attract even more visitors. Today Blackpool is still a popular **seaside resort**.

Tourism: a seaside town

Why did Blaenavon grow?

Blaenavon

Blaenavon is a town in South Wales. Many visitors to Blaenavon go there to see the Big Pit, a coalmine which is open to visitors. The Big Pit is a big clue about why Blaenavon grew!

Blaenavon grew because of mining in the 1800s. Coal and iron ore were found on the sides of a valley, and people began to make iron there. Soon the coal on the valley sides was used up, so miners had to go deep underground to get the coal.

Visitors can get a tour of the coal mines at the Big Pit Mining Museum.

Mining: coal

The town of Blaenavon grew up along the valley. There were **terraced houses** for the miners and their families. There were schools, shops, chapels and places to meet.

Now there is no mining in Blaenavon, but the town is a World Heritage Site because it shows how life used to be for the miners.

Why did Crewe grow?

Crewe is a town in Cheshire. Before 1840 there was only a small **hamlet** and scattered farms where Crewe is now. There was also a railway junction, the place where several train lines cross. One of the railway companies wanted to build a place to make and repair steam trains. What could be a better place than an important railway junction? The town of Crewe was born!

One of the old steam trains built in Crewe.

The railway works began in 1843. It became bigger and bigger, and more and more people went to work there. The railway company built nearly everything in the town. It built schools, churches and houses. It laid out the streets and parks. Crewe became world famous for the trains which were made there.

The railways are a big clue about the growth of Crewe. Crewe was a town which grew because of the railways. Thousands of people still travel through Crewe by train every day, but the trains are now powered by diesel engines and electricity.

An aerial view of Crewe.

Transport: a railway town

Why did Cambridge grow?

Cambridge

Cambridge is a city in Cambridgeshire. It is famous for its **university**, but at first there was another reason why it began to grow. It started to grow up around a ford where the River Cam could be crossed.

People have lived in Cambridge for over two thousand years. Iron Age people, Romans, Saxons and Normans all lived in Cambridge. William the Conqueror built a castle there, and the castle mound can still be seen.

Castle Mound

The first college of the university was built in 1284. Over the years more colleges were added, and the university became more and more important. Large numbers of people went to Cambridge to study.

Many of the college buildings are very beautiful, and tourists come from all over the world to see them. Many people still study in Cambridge.

So the college buildings are clues to why Cambridge grew. It grew because it became a world famous centre of learning.

Students who have just finished their studies.

Learning: a university town

Why did Milton Keynes grow?

Planners advertised Milton Keynes as having everything: modern facilities and lovely countryside.

Milton Keynes is a town in Buckinghamshire. It grew because in 1967 **planners** and politicians decided that a new town was needed.

The town is built around some older villages and some small towns, so it is not all brand new. One of the villages was called Milton Keynes, and gave its name to the new town.

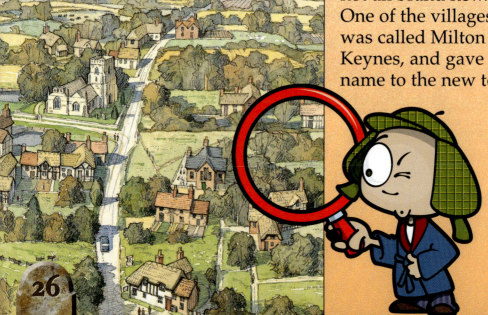

The planners designed Milton Keynes carefully. They wanted the new town to have plenty of homes and jobs so that people could work in the town itself. The roads were designed to cut down on traffic jams. New schools were built, and lots of trees and bushes were planted to make the town a good place to live.

In the middle of the new town a big new shopping centre was built. There are also offices, entertainments, car parks and a station. In the centre of Milton Keynes there are no old buildings at all! This gives us a clue about how Milton Keynes grew. It was designed and built as a new town.

The Shopping Centre

Milton Keynes Theatre

Xscape Entertainment Centre

Planning: a new town

Be a town detective!

Here are some things to look for:

🏠 Start with the name of the town. It may tell you something about the town. For instance, if the name ends with 'ham' or 'ton', the town may have begun as a Saxon village.

🧺 Does the town have a market? If it does, see if you can find out when it began, and where the stallholders and shoppers come from.

✝ Does the town have a castle, a cathedral, or an old church? What can you find out about it?

🏭 Does the town have any factories? Is it famous for any products? See what you can find out about your town's industries.

If you can investigate some of these questions you may find out quite a lot about the town and why it grew. And if you can visit the local studies section of the library, you should be able to find out even more!

If towns could talk, they would tell interesting and complicated stories about how they grew!

Glasgow, a city on the River Clyde

Blackpool, a seaside resort

Bradford, a town which grew because of the wool industry

Melton Mowbray, a market town

Cambridge, a university town

Crewe, a town which grew because of the railways

Blaenavon, a town which grew because of mining

Bath, an historic spa

Milton Keynes, a new town

Canterbury, a centre of religion

Glossary

alehouse a house where ale (beer) is sold

cathedral a church that contains a bishop's throne

ford a place where you can wade across water

Glaswegian a person from Glasgow

goods things that are bought and sold

hamlet a small village

inn a hotel or public house for travellers

iron ore sand or gravel containing iron

merchant someone who buys and sells goods

monastery a house for monks

pier a walkway running out into the sea

pilgrim someone who travels to a holy place for religious reasons

planner someone who controls the way land is developed

spinner someone who makes thread out of wool or cotton

stonemason someone who cuts stone

terraced house a house joined to other houses in a row

university a place to study

weaver someone who makes thread into cloth

World Heritage Site a place that is protected because of its historical importance

Index

Big Pit, the	20	market	4, 6, 8–9, 15, 28
Bath	16–17	Melton Mowbray	8–9
Blackpool	18–19	Milton Keynes	26–27
Blaenavon	20–21	mining	6, 20
Bradford	12–13		
buildings	25, 27, 28	planner	26, 31
		port	6, 10, 11
Canterbury	14–15		
Cambridge	24–25	railway	19, 22–23
cathedral	6, 14, 28, 31	river	10-11, 12, 24
Clyde, River	10–11	Romans	14, 16, 24
coal	11, 20	Saxons	14, 24
Crewe	22–23	seaside	18–19
		ships	11
factories	3, 13, 28		
ford	12, 24, 31	tourists	15, 17, 25
		town	2, 4–5, 6–7, 28
Glasgow	10–11, 31		
goods	8, 10, 31	university	6, 24, 25, 31
hamlet	22, 31	village	4, 12
houses	8, 17, 21, 23,		
		weavers	4, 12, 31
industry	6, 11, 12–13, 28	William the Conqueror	24
iron ore	11, 20, 31	World Heritage Site	17, 21, 31